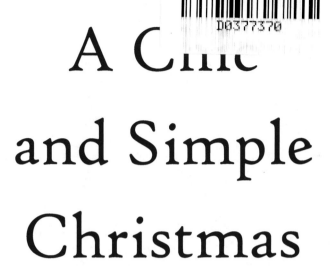

A Chic and Simple Christmas

Celebrate the holiday season with ease and grace

FIONA FERRIS

ISBN-13: 978-1539954941
ISBN-10: 1539954943

CONTENTS

Introduction

If you're anything like me, you love to cultivate a chic and elegant way of being and celebrate the joy of living, no matter the time of year. During the holidays however, it seems that chicness is harder to maintain and can fall by the wayside as Christmas Day draws closer.

The irony that this 'should' be the most joyous and happiest month on our calendar doesn't escape me, as we pile more and more onto our already sagging shoulders. Work is busy, there are social commitments, gifts to buy, our budget to balance and at least two families to accommodate; not to mention the politics if anyone has fallen out.

There is just something about the holidays that seems to push our buttons. I think part of it is that we remember how much fun it was when we were children; that gloriously giddy feeling of the big day approaching and the excitement of anticipating what Santa would leave at the end of our bed.

Now that we are grown-ups we have a lot more responsibility and it seems that we have to climb the mountain of December before we're allowed to rest, relax and enjoy Christmas. And even then, Christmas Day isn't really a day off when you're cooking, entertaining and cleaning up, is it?

So just how can we bring about a calm and serene feeling to really enjoy and fully participate in this magical time?

This is something I seem to struggle with every year; the divide between the chic and simple Christmas of my dream life, and, well, real life. Finally, I decided that a plan, a chic vision if you will, was in order so I could survive the holidays with my chic-self intact. And not just survive them, but master the art of living well during the holiday season.

Something I realised I crave, at any time of the year but especially during the holidays is *simplicity*. I know there are folk who love the frenetic energy of the holiday season, but I am not one of them. It stresses me out and makes me snappy with my husband. That's not what I want the Christmas season to be about.

I wrote this book because I wanted to create a sort of chic toolkit that would help me navigate the Christmas season with ease and grace. Too often in the past I've looked forward to Christmas *so much* only to practically shipwreck myself on the (tinsel-covered) rocks because I expected everything to magically work itself out and for others to be able to read my mind of what a perfect Christmas looks like. That's totally reasonable, right?

No matter the time of year you are reading this book, whether it is the second week in December or the middle of April, I believe it's never too soon to start thinking about your ideal Christmas holiday season. By this I don't mean start your gift shopping; I mean really work out for yourself what you'd like to experience and start creating and planning that.

I've studied personal development for long enough now to know that you have to *create* what you want, and move towards it with intention and purpose versus the way I used to do it; which was daydream and hope and then be disappointed, resulting in me getting grumpy with everyone and overeating to soothe myself.

I'm not talking about controlling others, that's not it at all. I've also tried to do *that* in the past, try and bend others to my way of thinking because I think my way is best (just a *little* bit arrogant, then). And really, isn't 'best' a matter of opinion anyway?

When I was first starting out in my own home as a twenty-something, I went along with what everyone else was doing and that was fine, it was the only way I knew. But as the years went by and I realized there were some parts of Christmas that really didn't make me feel festive and joyous, I started to change the way I did things.

After all, we're free people and have the right to live our life in exactly the way we please. Some might say this is selfish, but to me it is one of the most unselfish things you can do. Going along with others ideas of a good time at the expense of what *you* desire will leave you resentful and burnt out.

How can you be a loving and giving person to others when you feel like that? I'll tell you from experience – it's extremely difficult and becomes even more so over time. If you do manage it, the feeling of unease will increase and eventually surface in other ways, whether it's exploding in frustration at inconvenient times, overeating, or other 'overs' such as medicating yourself with a soothing glass of wine or going shopping and spending money that you don't have.

Personally, I was the Queen of Sugar. Give me chocolate, give me sweets/lollies/candy. Just give it to me, now! And I don't know about you, but sugar, even though it's nice at the time; afterwards makes me fat, grumpy and with low energy. Mmmm, so chic...

Shall we start planning for the first of many very happy holiday seasons we are to have from now on? Let me take you through what I've worked out.

Chapter 1.

Choose what a chic Christmas season feels like for you

What would your ideal Christmas be like? To start with, think of words, feelings and things to include and write them down. If there is something that bothers you and your ideal holiday season wouldn't include it, write down the opposite.

When I was doing this, I made sure that I focused *only* on what my ideal Christmas would be like if there were no outside factors. Naturally we do all have outside factors, but to start off with don't take those into account at all, so that you aren't influenced. In the end, you don't have to go with every single thing on your list, but starting out with what would be *parfait* (perfect!) for you, gives you something to work towards.

It is actually rather fun designing your ideal Christmas season experience because you really can go to town; there are no limits on your imagination. For me:

My Ideal Christmas Holiday Season

- I feel peaceful and happy

- I don't have that much to do, and what I do have is organized so it's easy

- I have plenty of free time to relax in between social times

- I am slim and healthy and feel vibrant and energetic

- I am a joy to be around

- I have plenty of time to make our home nice

- I have plenty of time to read books

- We have a balance of going out for Christmas outings and the peacefulness of staying in

- We have things to look forward to after Christmas as well

Can you sense a theme of what I'm craving during the holiday season? I'm sure I'm not alone either; I get the feeling that many of us could use a little more time, a lot more peace and a lot less commercialism at Christmas.

Using the above list of my ideal Christmas, I started on a big list outlining my ideal *chic and simple* Christmas. These two words were what I wanted my Christmas to be like, but for you, choose whatever words resonate best with you, and make sure to include your name in your list name. Whenever I do this, it always makes my list more appealing to me and I am more inspired (that's why advertisers love to personalise their emails to you!)

For example, you might come up with:

- Tracy's beachy and relaxed Christmas

- Stephanie's simple and sophisticated Christmas

- Karen's Parisian chic Christmas

- Kristi's old-fashioned Italian family Christmas

It's fun to work with a theme so choose one that really excites you. Ideas will start flowing so brainstorm everything you can think of that would make your dream Christmas come alive. Don't be practical; just write down everything that pops into your head.

One tip: if you're having trouble coming up with answers, reword the statement as a question. Our minds love a good question and immediately get to work. Here's mine:

Fiona's chic and simple Christmas

- Decide that I *want* a chic and simple Christmas and let those words guide me

- No gifts – good wishes and love are exchanged instead

- Low-key family get-togethers filled with fun and happiness

- Make sure the lead-up to Christmas is a time of peace – by being pared down and organized; and by thinking peaceful thoughts and letting that flow through to how I am

- Reconsider obligations that I know will drain me

- Be organised with lists to get through everything I'm planning for my ideal Christmas

- Make sure that I have plenty of energy and am in good health by eating well

- Allow plenty of down-time to recharge

- Have chic and simple Christmas décor that suits my style and doesn't take too much time to put up or take down

- Not try to control anyone else – just sort myself out and let everyone else be; it's not my business what others do or think

- Think of anyone I want to reach out to during the holiday season

- Remember all the ways in which I am blessed

- Go on a fabulous tropical vacation afterwards

Next is to note down what you love about Christmas and what stresses you about Christmas, to work out what you need to change:

What I really enjoy about Christmas:

- Watching Christmas movies

- Listening to Christmas music while I'm doing things at home

- The festive lead-up: viewing lit-up homes, special outings

- Seeing Christmas trees in people's windows, lights twinkling

- The fact that most people are happy and chatty because it's a fun season

- Spending time with my family

What stresses me out about Christmas:

- Gift-giving

- Other peoples' expectations and obligations on me

- Packing everything you ever wanted to finish into one month

- Busy at work so home gets neglected

- I sometimes eat badly so I gain weight and feel unmotivated and unenergized

What I am neutral about/doesn't worry me at Christmas:

- Having Christmas lunch or dinner at our place

- Accommodating both sides of the family

Before I made this list, I always wondered just how I could look forward to the holiday season *so much* but then become so stressed and grouchy because it didn't match my ideal (movie-style!) dream. People had their own agendas and, incredibly, they didn't miraculously go along with my (unvoiced) plans. The cheek!

I honestly thought that I must live in fairy-land because I simultaneously loved and intensely disliked Christmas, but seeing these lists just meant there were parts I liked and parts I didn't like.

With the help of these lists, I now see where things weren't aligning. Having everything down on paper and out of my head, helped me see just where the disconnects lay. Perhaps you are the same? Maybe just with different items on each list?

For example, you might really dislike Christmas music, so that would be on your 'stress' list. The thought of Christmas approaching and all that Christmas music in malls might make you shudder. So you may choose to embrace the holiday season by enjoying decorating your home and playing beautiful classical music, and shopping at small independent stores or online to avoid 'mall muzac'.

To create the holiday season of my movie dreams, I used the concept that I apply to other areas of my life so successfully, and that is to partake in the items on my love list and figure out what to do with the rest, to minimise or eliminate them.

This meant I could relax and enjoy what I loved about Christmas – making it a chicly customized holiday season. And I can only have my chicly customized Christmas if I sit down and nut out just what's important and what's not; what stresses me and what makes me happy. It sounds so simple but it's taken me quite some time – years in fact – to get to this point.

Don't think that some people won't be unhappy about you doing this, because they will. Many people are uneasy with change and they may feel threatened when they see you making different choices. You don't have to make it too scary for them though, and there's no reason to be deliberately annoying, but there's also no reason to continue to do things year after year that hold no joy for you, and may even cause you resentment and stress.

You can also choose to present some of the changes in ways which could help them 'soak in' a little easier.

Christmas style versus your personal style

Here lies another conundrum to work through on our journey to our ideal Christmas.

Personally, I love the thought of Christmas and a beautifully decorated house, however in my own home I become claustrophobic with too much stuff around me. I love an elegant and simple decor style *and* I also like to make things easy for myself (spending days decorating our home only to take it all down a month later does not sound like fun to me).

There's another thing too that we need to face: there's plenty of tacky Christmas stuff out there; it is enough make a stylish woman squirm. Thankfully there also many elegant and simple ideas around, from the whitewashed, wooden and icy pastels of Scandinavian holiday style to traditional Ralph Lauren tartan and fir boughs. No matter your colour scheme at home, there will be something you can find – or make – to enhance your décor *and* bring a bit of festive light to your surroundings.

At our house, I like things kept simple and elegantly rustic. I feel most at peace with light to medium neutral tones in various textures, with plenty of natural elements to help me feel grounded. To enhance and pep up my beloved neutrals, I also love a dash of red. To be honest I love a dash of red all year round, but at Christmas it's especially nice.

I had a fun thought on how best to describe my approach to holiday decorating (and to put it in the best light, not just 'Fiona's lazy').

You know how in Paris; most people live very centrally in apartments? Sure, they might have a window-box or two or even a small terrace with potted red-orange geraniums, but Paris is famous for her residents enjoying public parks almost as their own back yard as they read, lie in the sun, play and kiss; enjoying their own company in the company of others.

Well that's how I feel about Christmas decorating. I love to read the glossy magazines with heavily decorated homes. I love to watch holiday movies with the perfect family home decked out entirely in a store's-worth of beautiful and perfect Christmas décor. I love to visit neighbourhoods that are famous for their homes being decorated and all lit up on the outside. I love the feeling that all these things give me. And I love going home to my own chic and simple lightly-decorated house.

I've decided to call this the Parisian approach to Christmas decor.

Declutter what doesn't fit your vision of a chic Christmas

The paring down of my Christmas décor is something I started a few years ago. I didn't have huge amounts, but each year I'd donate something that no longer felt right for me.

One year I decluttered all the purple decorations I inexplicably had. I don't quite know what I was thinking when I bought these, because I'm not a fan of purple and it's not a very Christmassy colour. I must have been caught in a weak moment and thought our tree needed a bit more pizzazz (it didn't). I now have a small and lovely assortment of Christmas tree ornaments in silver, gold and red.

Charity stores are always keen for any kind of Christmas decorations in good order, either to decorate with or sell to raise money.

This year, I donated our faux tree and a faux wreath. The tree was quite small, but still took time to unpack and assemble, then decorate. Even after all that effort, I didn't like the look of it. *Simplicity* was not a word I would use to describe it; *hot mess* felt more appropriate.

One of my favourite charity stores gladly accepted it.

I did keep our decorations because we might want to have a real Christmas tree from time to time. I like to travel light in life and décor, and Christmas is no exception it seems!

Candles and a few select decorations is how I'm decorating for Christmas this year.

I have candles flickering on our coffee table every night no matter the season, mostly tealights in pretty holders. At Christmas, I take the opportunity to amp it up. This year I bought a new Christmas-themed candle glass.

There are many inexpensive and stylish candle holders that can be as opulent or simple as you like. They don't have to be Christmas-themed either, so that you can use it at other times. I just felt like I *needed* a Christmas candle holder this year.

Our new candle holder is made of red glass with a mirrored inside and cut-outs of a Christmas tree, reindeer and snowflakes. I promise it's more tasteful than it sounds. Yes, it's summer here in New Zealand at Christmas-time, but I still love the thought of a cold and snowy Christmas season.

You don't have to have specialised Christmas decorations either. A look that I love is to display different sizes of white or cream pillar candles clustered on a silver- or gold-toned tray. By adding a few of your smaller Christmas decorations such as pieces of tinsel or beading, tiny wrapped parcels and shiny baubles around the candles makes this a pretty and low-cost tableau.

A *chic and simple Christmas* summary

To summarize, here are my top tips on how to choose what a chic Christmas season looks like for you:

- Decide how you want your Christmas to feel this year and create an exciting and fun theme for yourself (no-one else even needs to know you have a Christmas theme, if you want to keep it private).

- Work out what you like and don't like about Christmas, and what you're neutral about. Use these lists to form your holiday season vision making sure you do plenty of 'likes' and work out a do-able way to minimize your 'don't likes'.

- Decorate your home in a way that makes you happy. Don't worry about what everyone else is doing whether it's your neighbour, your mother or someone on Pinterest. Choose to do something because it inspires you and feels good.

Chapter 2.

Prepare for a chic holiday season

From December 1ˢᵗ, give yourself the gift of feeling new and fresh by beginning the month with a clean slate. Allow yourself to feel excited for the holiday season and promise yourself that it is going to be the best and most fun one yet.

Hold onto the glittery and sparkling Christmas feeling you have inside, when inevitable thoughts crop up reminding you of all that you still have to get through over the coming weeks. Yes, there's work, social engagements, shopping and food preparation; but you have to do that anyway, so you may as well feel good. Remember, Christmas starts as an inside job.

Clear all non-essentials from December

The thing with Christmas and why so many of us find it a stressful season, is that Christmas comes *on top* of everything else we'd normally be doing. There are also less days to complete everything, which is why we can end up feeling crunched for time in December.

Something I've found really helpful, is to look at all the things that fall in December and decide what really needs to be there. Of course anything Christmas-related does, but what I also found were routine things that could have been done any other month of the year. They were in December just because they'd always been there. It's easy enough to re-schedule them to fall in another month so that's what I did, and they will then recur in a non-December month in the following years.

As an example of this is our six-monthly Warrant of Fitness safety check on our car. It fell right on New Year's because we originally bought our car in early July. This meant we'd usually do our safety check earlier in December because our garage was closed down over the

Christmas and New Year period. Even this was inconvenient though, when there were already so many other things to do in December. We decided to have our next Warrant of Fitness check in November, a month early, and now it's out of the way before December starts, this year and every year.

Along the same lines I never book routine medical appointments in December or January and try to have my final hair appointment for the year in the first week of December.

You might think examples such as these are inconsequential, but all the little things add up. Rescheduling non-urgent appointments either earlier or later than the Christmas season, means there is more time, energy – and money – for the fun things such as holiday parties we are invited to, getting organized for a post-Christmas vacation if we have one planned, and looking forward to a serene and enjoyable holiday season.

Get shopping out of the way

This may sound non-Christmassy when advertisements show happy families joking and laughing as they stroll down the snowy street carrying glossy shopping bags, but tell me, has your Christmas shopping ever looked like that? Mine hasn't.

More often it means you've left work already tired and you still have to go home and cook dinner. You arrive at the mall for late-night shopping and it's a *zoo* – you can't believe how many people are there and unfortunately you are one of them tonight. You try to buy what you need and get out quickly, but it still takes too long and you end up *hangry*. To soothe your hunger and your nerves, you scoff down chocolate all the way home... Yes, that is what my Christmas shopping used to look like.

If you're not the sort of person who enjoys visiting malls at the best of times, shopping in December is your worst nightmare; I know it is mine. It seems that many stores are on sale well before Christmas now, so there's no reason to wait for bargains. I decided to try and have all of my gift purchases completed in November.

Of course there may well be last minute items as well as perishable foods to purchase in December, but that's a breeze compared with trying to buy all your gifts much closer to Christmas Day. I know there are loads of organized people who already do this, but I got how well this worked when we had an extremely early Christmas one year, because we were going to be away for Christmas Day.

To prepare, I had all my Christmas shopping completed and wrapped early. I thought I may as well do both sides of the family at once, and found that I was so relaxed and able to keep on top of the everyday things; it was marvellous.

It was certainly more relaxing than my usual method of relying on a deadline (in this case the 25th of December) to act as a sort of funnel meaning I became more stressed and frantic as Christmas Day came closer.

Keep yourself healthy

I know from experience that it is very easy to let self-care fall by the wayside in December. For me it's a combination of being busy with additional tasks, along with the 'letting loose' feeling of Christmas coming up when I treat myself more often.

I will go to bed a little later, miss a few daily walks, eat more goodies than I usually do and slack a bit, both at home and work because I am feeling in a festive holiday mood. It's not that I plan to do all these things and then plan to feel bad about myself, it just... happens.

I used to think self-discipline was boring and only for uptight people, but guess what, when I tried it, it felt amazing! It wasn't even *that* hard either; like a lot of things it was simply a matter of making a decision and following through. Instead of feeling trapped, I felt quite free. Why? Because I felt *so good*. I hadn't put on weight, I had loads of energy and I was on top of my tasks and chores (which didn't even feel like tasks and chores because they were so easy).

I admit that even though I did so well last Christmas, it doesn't mean I naturally carried on. I certainly have my times of being really 'on' and naturally highly organized and energized, then I have my times of quite low energy where I just want to curl up and read a good book with a bar of Cadburys nearby.

I've come to accept this about myself though and know that it's okay to rest when I'm not feeling as motivated. During these times I treat myself with lots of reading, comforting clothing in soft, natural fibres, plenty of protein with my meals, not too many carbs (whilst still having a few treats on the weekend) and plenty of rest and relaxation; without feeling guilty or like I *should be doing something*. Maybe it's a perfectionist thing?

Part of being organized in December is 'banking' easy meals in our freezer so we aren't tempted by takeaway meals. I'm all for a takeout meal when you're in the mood and it's planned for as a weekend treat, but not if it's a Tuesday night and neither of us feels like cooking. I don't enjoy a takeaway meal as much in this situation because it feels like I'm just being lazy, and not prioritizing my health.

Some of my favourite meals to cook double (or even quadruple is quite easy since it's just the two of us; we then get one meal that night and three for the freezer) are:

- Meatloaf

- Casserole

- Bolognese

- Nachos mince

- Cottage Pie

These form the basis of some of our evening meals, then it's just a matter of adding fresh vegetables. I found that when we were getting takeaways it wasn't that we wanted them, we just couldn't think what else to cook that was fast and easy. You do need to defrost a freezer meal ahead of time, but even then there are microwaves to do a last minute defrost (I like to reheat in a frying pan, pot or the oven though; the flavour and texture is much nicer).

I alternate made-ahead meals with freshly cooked meals so we don't get bored with the same thing.

Declutter in advance

Decluttering your home in preparation for the holiday is such a nice way to begin the festive season. Your home will feel nice for Christmas *and* you will be ready for what is to come, because even when you try to have a minimalist Christmas, there is *always* more, don't you find?

By decluttering, you will give others a chance to buy items you have donated; giving the charity their money and giving someone else the ability to gift some of your lovely items for Christmas presents. You might not realise it, but there are many for whom charity shops are their only option when it comes to buying gifts.

This thought alone helps me release decluttered items that I am resisting donating because they are 'too good' or I spent money on them.

Simplify before the holidays

December is a time that, if you've not been simplifying things during the year, can snowball (no pun intended). One such example that comes to mind for me is the many email lists I used to belong to. I didn't want to unsubscribe from any of them because I thought I'd miss out on a bargain, so I just used to delete them as they came in.

Going into the holiday season as I'm sure you know, retail stores become *extremely prolific* in their marketing campaigns. One day I'd had enough and made a blanket decision to unsubscribe from all the sales emails as they came through.

I admit I did have thoughts of 'what if they have 'half price everything' and I don't know?' but I stuck to my decision and it felt *so good* not to wade through so many junk emails in my Inbox. I also trusted that the Universe would let me now about something if I needed it.

Nowadays when I do decide that I want to buy a certain item, I know it's something I want from my own thoughts rather than seeing a bargain and *needing* it even though I had managed to live without it before that. I do my research and also ask the Universe to help me find exactly what I want at the best possible price. I always find what I need and once I've purchased it, I stop looking. I do the best job at the time and trust that I received what I needed.

After the great email unsubscribe my Inbox is more serene and I haven't been spending money (and time) on buying stuff that I'll likely need to declutter in the future anyway. You won't believe the calmness of opening your Inbox in the morning to find a few personal emails and *no marketing*. It's blissful.

A *chic and simple Christmas* summary

To summarize, here are my top tips on how to prepare for a chic holiday season:

- Feel excited for your upcoming fun holiday season which promises to be full of love and happiness – because it all starts with you, and you already know that your heart is festive and generous.

- Clear the decks come December 1st. Keep this month free of as many routine obligations as possible to give yourself space to organize and enjoy.

- Shop as early as possible – try and have your gift shopping done by the end of November.

If you can have it wrapped by then, even better. You will be happy about your efforts three weeks later, I promise you.

- Prioritize your health – this is not a time to fall into the seductive arms of convenience foods and sugary treats. You need nutrition, hydration and rest for this busy time.

- Stock your freezer in advance for quick and healthy meals in December.

- Prepare for incoming goodies at Christmas by decluttering. Even just a little bit will make your home feel nice. You will also feel doubly blessed at the thought of your decluttered items ending up being a loved Christmas gift from a person who is not as lucky as you are.

- Unsubscribe from junk emails and be very selective about the ones you keep. They have to earn their place in your Inbox (and your consciousness). Do they enrich your life? If not, they go.

Chapter 3.
Christmas giving

What starts out as a way for people to show appreciation for their loved ones often seems to turn into a less than fun part of the holiday season.

For starters, there are:

- Gifts that are not to your taste which means they are donated or thrown away if you don't want to clutter your home with them.

- Wasting of money on gifts that aren't going to be used.

- Exchanging gifts of money – if they are the same value, then what's the point?

- If you ask people what they want as a gift and they ask you, yes you'll not waste your money buying something they don't like and they to you, but again, if you know what you're getting, is there any point in swapping gifts?

- Exchanging gifts with people who are known for being penny-pinchers.

- Not knowing what to give to people – I find men quite hard to buy for.

- Being sent in pursuit of a very specific and hard-to-find gift (I see this often in our retail store; sometimes the item they are after literally does not exist).

I know it doesn't seem very festive to bring all this up, but it truly shows everything I dislike about how the gift-giving tradition has evolved.

Gifting vs non-gifting

As families grow bigger, I do wonder why we all rush around buying each other gifts, when we already have more than we could ever use. We then spend our January not only paying our credit cards, but decluttering our excess as well. There's something quite dysfunctional and obnoxiously wasteful about that, would you agree?

In the past, I exchanged gifts with immediate and extended family, friends and sometimes work colleagues. Over the years as I gained confidence in choosing what I allowed in my own life, I asked people if they were happy to exchange a card or even just a Christmas email and good wishes instead of gifts. I found that most people I approached with this seemed happy about it, and often quite relieved.

After all, what do we really 'need' when we live in a first-world country with many of us having more than we could ever need or use, and our more pressing problem being how to declutter than not having enough.

I am always looking around at what I can declutter in order to live a streamlined life full of ease. A streamlined life full of ease? Now *that* would be the ultimate Christmas present and yay, that's exactly what I'm getting, by streamlining gifts.

If I could choose, we wouldn't exchange gifts at Christmas, instead giving each other love, time spent and good wishes. I'd definitely enjoy this more and I'm sure everyone's stress levels would decrease markedly, both before (shopping) and after (paying for them) the big day has gone.

If you do plan to change the way you give gifts, make sure people have plenty of notice, because some people choose to shop during the year. You could even broach the subject on Christmas Day for the next year by saying something like, 'Phew, look at all these gifts. I don't know how we're going to fit them into our house. Who's up for trying that minimalist thing next year? Or a Secret Santa, or maybe buy for the children only?', then listen for others' views on the subject.

My siblings and I did this a few years ago and now we don't exchange Christmas gifts at all. We buy for my nieces and nephew and I have to say that this trimmed-down-gifting feels better to me. In case you're wondering, we have just as much fun on Christmas day and we don't seem to miss those gifts.

My husband and I don't exchange gifts either. I used to think this was unromantic but now I love it, and so does he. We are both quite sensible spenders and it's nice to know that if we see something at any time of the year that we need or would simply like to have, we can purchase it. That is far more fun to me than a rigid 'official gifting time' of Christmas.

With my extended family, all the cousins stopped doing gifts a long time ago because we often weren't all in the same place on Christmas Day. This year however, we are all getting together, so a $20 Secret Santa is planned. Everyone takes one gift and leaves with one gift and it promises to be a lot of fun to see what people have found for their $20.

Children are different, and I still give gifts to nieces and nephews; it's just adults' gifts that have been changed. I certainly don't need an ornament, box of chocolates or a book from someone to know that they love me. The most fun for me is to get together with family and have a jovial meal where we can wear paper hats, eat delicious food and enjoy each other's company. The children open their gifts and the adults can have a good old catch-up.

Another aspect of gift-giving that stresses me is the waste. I'm all for spending money if it's something you or someone else needs or wants. But all too often, Christmas gifts are generic to be safe, or bought at the last minute out of desperation only to be left as another piece of clutter or donated to a charity shop because they are not to the recipient's taste. What a waste of both the giver's time and money; and I'm certain that's not what the spirit of Christmas is all about.

Some retail businesses would not survive if it wasn't for the consumer frenzy in December. Our business is a bit different being a shoe store but even we see a sales bump in December – yes, people give shoes as gifts, and no, I'm not looking a gift horse in the mouth. I do, however, see rather a lot of frantic people shopping for gifts and it doesn't look like they're having fun.

Every year Christmas advertising seems to get bigger and bigger and starts earlier – I've seen retail stores bring out Christmas products in late September! We buy into this gigantic Christmas bonanza and it's all in aid of transferring your hard-earned money into the bank accounts of the malls. If you're happy about that, please, feel free to carry on as you are.

But if you're like me and this acceleration towards consumerism and excess makes you uneasy, there is another choice and that's to embrace the bits you like about Christmas and opt out of the rest.

Easier said than done, I know; so just how can we have the possibly awkward conversation with extended family members? Firstly, make sure you are on the same page as your spouse. Talk it over with them first so that you are both happy with your decision and can put on a united front.

Next, think about how you're going to bring it up with those concerned. Both sides of my family are good on email, so one of us might start a group email saying something like 'hey, what's everyone's thoughts on gifts for next year? Shall we try something different? Here are my thoughts...'

If you have family members further removed that you don't want to enter into discussion with; either a brief telephone conversation or an email letting them know your decision is probably best. Perhaps: 'Just letting you know that we are doing things a little bit differently from now on. We're opting out of all gifts except for under tens', as an example; worded with whatever you decide to do.

Talking with friends recently about this very thing, one lady's Christmas gifting practice that made a lot of sense to me went as follows: children receive gifts up until the age of seventeen, when they are then welcomed into the adults $20 Secret Santa for those aged eighteen and over. Rather than being kicked out of children's gifts, they have 'graduated' into the adult's club. I thought this was an excellent plan.

Gift alternatives

I have not tried this type of thing yet, but have heard many different people talk about the things they do that don't involve joining a thousand other people at a shopping mall.

Great examples I've heard of include:

- Swapping time i.e. a housework bee, babysitting if you both have young children, a day of decluttering or help with a wardrobe overhaul.

- Homemade gifts such as biscuits/cookies, cakes and sweets; knitted or sewn items; preserves, jams, jellies and chutney.

- Giving away jewellery or family china to members of your family. My nana did this as she grew older. One Christmas, she gave my sister and I a teacup, saucer and plate set from her collection. I only have a few pieces like this but they really elevate teatime when I use them.

- Giving experiences instead of items: once you start on this line of thought, you'll realize just how many options there are for gift experiences with such items as movie tickets, restaurant or hotel bookings, car racing, tickets to concerts, massage/ facial/ manicures, sky dives, bungee jumps, a luxury car experience, professional portrait, wine tasting with a professional or a helicopter ride.

Charitable giving

I do often gift to charities at Christmas-time, but mostly prefer to spread my giving year round. I have weekly automatic payments to two animal charities – one is a local cat shelter and the other is a rural animal sanctuary for bigger animals such as chickens, pigs, goats and ponies etc.

I feel happier about this than giving only at Christmas because not only does it spread the cost over a year, but it's one less thing off my plate in December and, if I don't get a chance to do anything extra in December, at least I'm doing something.

A *chic and simple Christmas* summary

To summarize, here are my top tips on holiday season gifting:

- Christmas is all about giving – gifts to loved ones, cheer and goodwill to people you come in contact with, and comfort to those with struggles. Don't forget to give to yourself as well.

- If gifts are a stress-point for you, have honest conversations with those you exchange gifts with to see if they are agreeable to a change. You may be surprised at how happy they are to do things differently.

- Consider other ways of exchanging gifts or even alternatives to gift giving.

- Remember your favourite charitable causes at Christmas or make a decision to give a smaller amount regularly, instead of a lump sum at Christmas when there are all sorts of other festive claims on your income.

Chapter 4.

Enjoying the holiday season

This is where the fun starts. From late November onwards, our chic minimal Christmas décor goes up and I start playing my favourite Christmas movies and music *without apology*.

For me, an important part of the holiday season is to have fun outings planned as well. As much as I love being at home, there's something about Christmas-time that makes me want to be a bit more social. I start thinking of a few things I'd like to do, maybe one a week.

It's so easy to say 'I'd love to go and see the lights on Franklin Road one night' but then nothing is arranged and we don't make it. Franklin Road is famous in the city where I live for being beautifully decorated each December. Families walk up and down both sides of the street to view the spectacularly decorated homes; there are coffee carts and it has a real festive atmosphere.

We've done this precisely once, whereas I'd love to do it every year. The trick to achieving this is to plan for a certain evening (weather permitting of course) and book it into the diary. It's the sort of outing my husband wouldn't choose himself, but when we'd been, he raved about it.

It's the same with Christmas movies. I'll see an advertisement and think 'that looks like fun, we must go' and then it never enters my head again. When I do take it a step further and ask my husband if he would enjoy it, then choose a night and book the tickets; that's when it becomes part of my reality. Not only does it increase the sense of Christmas, but we also have a fabulous evening out that creates holiday season memories for us.

Going to Starbucks for one of their seasonal hot drinks is another Christmas tradition I love.

I don't often go there during the year, but there's something about their Christmas coffee menu that appeals. I think I *am* quite susceptible to marketing! Never mind that I might really think these drinks are overpriced and kind of kitsch; I love going there and ordering a Peppermint Mocha or whatever their current seasonal offering is, and enjoying it in a cheery red cup.

It's not just about going out either. There are loads of things I love to do at home to bring about the magical feeling of Christmas. Christmas movies are one of my favourite at-home seasonal treats. We have a small library of Christmas DVDs including:

- Christmas with the Kranks

- National Lampoon's Christmas Vacation

- The Family Stone

- Love Actually

- The Holiday

- Bad Santa (so low-class, but so funny)

- Four Christmases (also quite tasteless, but it's one of my favourites)

My first holiday movie this season was a terrible Tori Spelling one that I watched on YouTube (*A Carol Christmas*). Gosh it was so bad it was almost good.

By the time I'd gotten through five of the eleven parts, I felt so invested that I continued through to the end (but really I was probably throwing good minutes after bad). The only saving grace was that it also featured William Shatner (possibly not one of his career highlights, but he was very funny as usual).

Now I can hear you thinking 'bad taste Christmas movies? That doesn't sound very chic to me'. And you're right, a dire Tori Spelling movie is not chic at all, but guess what? I've forgiven myself long ago for having my slightly tacky side. Even though I love to dream of all things chic and French, I also love my guilty pleasures.

I've heard that the classic French woman will blend a little bit of bad taste into her wardrobe to stop it becoming too staid. Veronique Vienne says in her 1993 cult book 'French Style' that their motive is to 'shock the matrons'. In clothing I suppose this would translate to a dash of leopard print (though this is practically a neutral now), a bright plastic bracelet or black lace on show; something unexpected or out of place.

So that's *obviously* what I'm doing here with my Tori Spelling movie, it's *très chic* don't you know!

I also love the feeling that holiday music gives me. I have a selection including:

- Jessica Simpson – *Happy Christmas* and *Rejoyce*

- Mariah Carey – *Merry Christmas*

- Sarah McLachlan – *Wintersong*

- Celine Dion – *These Are Special Times*

- Hayley Westenra – *Christmas Magic*

- Michael Bublé – *Christmas*

- Kelly Clarkson – *Wrapped in Red*

- Idina Menzel – *Holiday Wishes*

- Lady Antebellum – *On this Winter's Night*

- Dean Martin, Frank Sinatra, Bing Crosby – all the classics, of course!

Look, I never said I had great taste in music either. It's true, I do love those pop Christmas albums alongside the more classical holiday options. To increase the class quotient though, Rat Pack Christmas songs are fabulous and this is one CD I can successfully sneak past my husband.

I play Christmas music when I'm at home by myself and also later in December in our shop. I never tire of it, it's just that my husband has a limit on how much he can handle (we work together), so I get my fix at home on a day off by myself. I always ask him once it clicks over to December, 'just let me know when I can start playing Christmas music in the shop'!

I have a Christmas Lite playlist too, which includes all of our Christmas music plus other music which dilutes it somewhat, and it means I can sneak Christmas music into our shop earlier.

If you're one of those people who absolutely cannot stand Christmas music, choose tracks for your December playlist that feel festive and put you in a relaxed and happy mood. Classical violin/ strings do this for me, as does sultry Buddha Bar and Hôtel Costes mixes; and Michael Bublé/ Harry Connick Jnr/ Jeremy Davenport jazzy/ lounge type music.

Working out how you'd love to experience the holiday season is all about creating little

Christmas markers that anchor you into the festive feeling. My examples may not spark off a desire in you, so choose to do things that make *you* happy.

What are some outings or activities that you've talked about doing during the holiday season that seem to get missed out each year?

If Christmas entertaining stresses you out

Some people love throwing parties; I'm not one of them. I much prefer my entertaining to be low-key and more intimate. My favourite way to host friends is to hold dinner parties for up to six in total. It's not too stressful for me to think about doing this. The menu is simple and yummy and I get plenty of time to converse.

What way of entertaining do you feel happiest with? It could be an elaborate Christmas Eve party at your home or it could be absolutely nothing. Whatever choice you make as right for you, be okay with it and uphold your boundaries.

I used to feel bad that I didn't throw parties, especially when an invite came from someone who seemed to hold them with ease and regularity. They're just not my thing though, and I can happily return the favour by inviting the party-throwers back for dinner at a later date.

The main thing I've learnt is not to let anyone else dictate what *you* do and how *you* feel about your choices. Make the decision with your spouse and then let people know what's happening.

Be extra gentle with yourself

With December being such a busy time of year, sometimes the best thing you can think of doing is hibernating away and enjoying cozy early nights and snuggling at home with a box set, so why not? Practicing exquisite self-care and recognizing when you are feeling a little burnt out will help you keep up your festive *joie de vivre*.

Personally, some years I go out more and some years less. I just go with what I feel like doing at the time and follow my desires. This practice never fails me; in fact, the times when I do go off the rails is when I ignore my inner requests for peace and quiet. Honor your own voice just as much as you would honor your loved ones.

Moving your body will help you feel well and cope with any seasonal stress too. I've never been a fan of exercise but even I can admit when I'm wrong; and I don't actually count my walks as exercise either, they are my *serenity-preservers*. I go at a moderate pace and walk anywhere from twenty to sixty minutes, depending on the day. I might walk from home or work and I might walk in exercise gear or my normal outfit (I do change my shoes though).

A walk loosens up my muscles and settles any creakiness and I feel so good when I arrive back, plus I get to listen to something inspiring on my iPod (that's really the main attraction for me). Currently I have a Christmas song playlist which, when set on random, intersperses with my podcasts which is quite fun. Hello to Fifi's Holiday Season Radio!

Extra *chic and simple Christmas* ideas

Here are ten additional ways to enjoy your December and get into the good feelings of the holiday season:

- Holiday baking: bake cookies to give out as little gifts.

- Research concerts, live shows or theatre at Christmas-time and attend one.

- Learn about different religious celebrations (I'm going to learn about Hanukkah this year, it's not as well known in New Zealand as in other countries).

- Get out the board games. Nothing says family holidays to me like board games and I love remembering how much fun they are.

- Buy a gift for yourself – is there something you've been wanting for ages? Ask for it to be gift-wrapped and put it under the tree from you to you.

- Remember what you loved to do as a child at Christmas and plan more of that.

- Email family and friends overseas to say hi and merry Christmas.

- Treat yourself to a holiday novel and snuggle down on the sofa – I discovered recently that there is such a genre. Karen Swan is one author I saw on our local bookstore shelf and her latest title 'Christmas on Primrose Hill' looked so appealing. There are loads of others too when you look them up on Amazon. Who knew!

- Paint your toenails a bright toffee-apple red and let them dry whilst enjoying a holiday movie with your feet up.

- Have a potluck street dinner if you know you neighbours well. Or even if you don't, why not hold an open house 'drinks and nibbles' for a few hours?

Chapter 5.
Christmas Day

Something I find really helpful is to keep my ideal chic Christmas vision in mind at all times. I like to have a mental walk-through of any special occasion, including Christmas Day, and make myself a plan.

I imagine what I've chosen to wear and the fact that I've given myself time to do my hair and makeup (simple, not elaborate, but I've taken care with it). I picture myself arriving with time to spare so that I am not rushing and rudely turning up late.

There are family members who I get along easily with and some who are not so easy. I choose to be around people I enjoy conversing with, and try to avoid the ones who test me. It's not anything too heavy and I am always polite, but as you know, you can't choose your family, so it's best for your self-preservation to manage family occasions as well as possible.

It's important for me to be a good guest or a good host too. I have chic mentors in the form of other family members who I turn to in my mind, when I'm working out what to do in a situation.

If you don't have any in real life, why not choose a person you don't know, but that you admire their style. A few for me would be Martha Stewart, Gossip Girl character Lily van der Woodsen or even Joan Collins, whom I love. I mean, you can't help but change your mode if you ask yourself 'how would Joan Collins handle this', right?

I also think about how and what I will eat and drink on Christmas Day. I used to be a champion nibbler and a sweet tooth and looked upon Christmas as a free-for-all where nothing I ate could make me put on weight or feel unwell. And the reality is, food tells the truth even when you don't to yourself. You might not write down everything in a calorie-counting notebook, but your body is still adding it all up.

It is the weight thing yes, but more than that it's the feeling of being in control and peacefulness around food that I seek. I don't seem to be the type of person who can eat one piece of candy and then wander away happily. No, that one piece of candy sets off a chain reaction where I want to eat the rest of the dish, all at once.

For me, I find it easier not to have any at all, which in turn I find easier to do when I remember why it doesn't agree with me in the first place and what I'd rather have instead (a slim, healthy body and peace of mind). I'm not always perfect but I'm getting better all the time, and it's just about changing the way I think.

The other wonderful thing about not nibbling through Christmas Day is just how good your Christmas dinner tastes – *so* much better. Nibbling before a meal blunts your appetite and when dinner is served it's almost annoying because it intrudes on your nibbling fun time. But the 'fun' is all an illusion, one that I've fallen for many times in the past.

With drinks, I'd have just the one glass of wine with my meal. Any more and I'd feel too sleepy. One Christmas, we had a champagne breakfast and I thought to myself, 'this is so much fun!' as my glass was refilled. That was my most wretched Christmas in history; I felt sleepy and out of sorts all day. Being slightly tipsy before mid-morning is not a good start to the day and I never did that again.

I don't drink at all now and haven't for quite a few years, but I still have to be careful with what I drink. If I have something very sugary such as fruit juice or soda, it can give me a headache, especially on an empty stomach. And if I have a sweet drink with my meal, my stomach gurgles with the sugar fermenting and I'm sure I don't digest as well. I find sparkling mineral water much kinder and it's still something fizzy in a flute for me.

I used to think the drink inside the glass was the festive part, but often it's the glassware itself. Think about it: part of the romance of a glass of special wine is the vessel it's poured into. If you poured a beautiful French burgundy into a plastic cup, I doubt it would be as enjoyable. I borrowed this concept and now sip my evening drink from an attractive glass.

It sounds like an inconsequential thing but it makes a huge difference. I sip my drink rather than gulp, simply because of the glass; it's automatic. At a social occasion such as

Christmas Day or a Christmas party, no-one questions what you are drinking when it's in a flute or wine glass; I feel just as much a part of the occasion (because I sometimes felt separate from everyone else when they were drinking and I wasn't).

The main thing on Christmas Day is to enjoy yourself, and as I have matured, I have come to realise that enjoying yourself does not mean eating and drinking everything you clap your eyes on. Rather, enjoying yourself means eating and drinking in a chic and moderate way. You will then feel well, convey elegance and have a good time.

Accommodating two or more families

Making sure that everyone feels included and that each side of the family is equally treated is important at Christmas.

I heard of one couple who didn't want to 'sacrifice' either family, so chose to see neither on Christmas Day, just each other. As much as I love it to be just the two of us, Christmas is a family day to me so we will always spend Christmas Day with either my family or my husband's family.

In recent years, we've been spending Christmas Day with my husband's family, and the next day with my family. We imaginatively named the second day our 'Boxing Day Christmas' (Boxing Day, held on the 26th December is largely a tradition of the English). Believe it or not, it's still fun to have Christmas two days in a row!

If you don't plan to have two Christmases in forty-eight hours, then turn-about is the fairest way to share Christmas Day in my opinion, especially if there is a considerable geographical distance between the two families.

If you're in the same town then it's reasonable to have lunch at one home and dinner at another. But if you do have to travel, you can have an early (or late) Christmas with one family and Christmas Day with the other.

Simple and relaxing

For the most part I like to keep things simple on Christmas Day. After a busy month working in our store, where we don't close until mid-afternoon on Christmas Eve, it's a treat just to be at home.

When we hold Christmas dinner at our place, the theme is simplicity and elegance. We have a traditional roast and something yummy for dessert.

If there are traditions you and your family really enjoy, carry on; but if you realise some traditions are becoming more of a bothersome burden, don't torture yourself – let them go.

There's no Christmas fairy waiting to tell you off if you don't do everything that previous generations in your family have done, or if your Christmas doesn't look like the picture-perfect movie version complete with a Golden Retriever dog.

If no-one in your family particularly likes turkey or any kind of a roast, why not do something completely different?

This year my husband's family are having an early Christmas get-together at a beautiful local park and we are all bringing portable gourmet food. It's easy, there's no tidying up apart from everyone packing up their picnic baskets, and being outside – as long as the weather holds – is so refreshing.

I do realize this is probably not an option in the Northern Hemisphere!

When you're a guest or have guests to stay

It's easy to get through a family occasion when you are in your hometown for Christmas, because you know you can go home to your own space afterwards. But what if you are visiting relatives and staying with them or they with you? How can you preserve your sanity and therefore your chicness?

Feigning tiredness (you may not have to feign) and going to your room is a great way to sneak in a bit of alone time. This is especially important for us introverts, who are easily drained by group gatherings or prolonged social occasions (no matter how enjoyable). If it is an all-day affair, you may feel that it is appropriate to 'take a nap'. It's actually quite acceptable to doze off on Christmas day or any other day of the holiday season.

Once you're in your room of course, you don't need to nap; you might journal, read a novel or work on a knitting project you've brought with you; only to emerge a little while later a completely new person.

If you are spending Christmas Day at someone's home and are feeling drained, you can find a quiet place to sit and close your eyes for a minute. You could pick up someone's gift book for a flick through, or find an elderly relative or someone. else who is taking some time out too, to sit with in companionable silence or for a relaxed chat.

I also like to keep up my daily walks no matter where I am. If anyone wants to come with me that's fine, but for the most part I go for a stroll by myself. I love to get out of the house and, if I'm away, enjoy walking different streets than when I'm at home.

What to wear?

In New Zealand, we don't tend to dress for the holidays as much as other countries do. It's not common here to have holiday sweaters (especially since it's summer, they'd need to be holiday tee-shirts), Christmas pyjamas or womenswear in sparkles and metallics.

It's still nice to feel festive and a little dressy though, so I always wear a nice dress on Christmas day. My opinion, which I got from my mother, is that it's not a day for jeans or even trousers (and I wear jeans a lot).

The ideal Christmas outfit also allows for comfort as it's often a long day with plentiful food and drink. For example, I wouldn't choose to wear anything tight-fitting on Christmas day. As much as I try to keep my posture and hold my torso straight, I do prefer to wear something that is a little more relaxed in fit.

Personally, I say *non* to Christmas jewellery and wearing red and green together. I do however like the colour red by itself, or paired with white or beige.

One of my friends has quite a bohemian/ fashiony style – she is amazing at putting vintage and charity shop finds together and always looks *très chic* no matter what she is wearing. Well, she also likes to have fun with her clothing, so during the holiday season you will see her wearing her Christmas skirt made from vintage linen Christmas tea-towels. And it looks really great on her!

For my simpler taste though, a flattering and comfortable dress and low heels or flats are what I love to spend my Christmas Day in.

In the Christmas of my dreams where I spend the holidays with my darling at our lodge in the French Alps, I wear cozy and elegant cashmere leggings and a long slim-line sweater with a pom-pom drawstring neck. Both are in the same blush-pink shade. Divine!

The reality for us in New Zealand though is that it is more likely to be rather warm, so I will save my cashmere fantasies for the winter months.

A *chic and simple Christmas* summary

To summarize, here are my top tips for a fun and relaxing Christmas Day:

- Make a plan for the day – what you'll wear, how you will be around relatives who trigger you, what you will eat and drink and *not* eat and drink.

- Keep your mystique. Listen more than you talk, ask questions of others and enjoy the chic feeling of not letting it all hang out. Be positive, and resist the urge to complain or gossip. If others do, either smile noncommittally until you can escape, or change the subject if you can.

- Be prepared for food pushers. If you are offered something to eat or drink that you don't want, say 'thank you, that sounds lovely, I'm good now but I might try some later on' or 'how delicious, I'll be sure to try that soon'.

- Watch out for self-sabotage, old patterns and old habits coming up. It's only because they are familiar to you, it doesn't mean you have to follow them. When confronted with snacks and sweets that you don't really want to indulge in, tell yourself 'in the past I ate those, but now I prefer to be chic and enjoy my Christmas dinner'. Then sip elegantly on your sparkling mineral water.

- Be extra gentle with yourself – Christmas Day can be highly charged and it doesn't have to be. I have a couple of mantras that I repeat to myself (quietly or silently) when I'm anxious. They are 'all is well' and 'I am safe today and always'. They are both very soothing.

- Take a group photo on Christmas day. It's fun to see these change year by year, and as much as everyone will grumble about having to get into place and that they hate having their photo taken, they will love receiving a copy. Be the person who makes this happen – be the bossy one!

- Keep it simple on Christmas Day – uphold traditions that you enjoy and skip the rest without guilt.

- Don't stress about family niggles. Let others be as they are, maintain your own boundaries politely, and simply keep away from those who trigger you.

Chapter 6.

Have exciting things to look forward to in the New Year

How I love January! It feels like a new start with no expectations, and you can really dive into refreshing your home as you tidy up after Christmas celebrations. It is also a time to say goodbye to houseguests and pack away any seasonal décor you have had displayed.

It's almost as if we need January to be peaceful, in order to breathe after the busyness of December. Even for those of us who intentionally keep our holiday season as simple as possible, it is a lovely feeling to sail into the smooth, clear waters of the New Year.

As you put away gifts, take the time to clear out any duplicates, and donate or throw out as appropriate. Clean and organize sections of your home as you go, and feel your energy levels rise as order is restored. I love to read my favourite homemaking blogs for inspiration when I'm doing this. HomeLiving.blogspot.com is one of my favourites.

If you are reluctant to pack away the feeling of Christmas too soon, why not play Christmas music as you clean up?

Many people will be away over this period. If you are at home, consider inviting friends around for dinner, who are also in town. It's great to see people who aren't family members after such a family-focused time, and you can swap funny stories from Christmas day (you *know* there will be some).

Be your own cheerleader

Another thing I love about January is the opportunity it provides to reflect on the previous year. In my journal I try to fill in at least one whole page, writing down fabulous things I've achieved, learned or created. If *you* aren't your own pep rally, why would anyone else be? No-one else needs to see your notes either, if this thought makes you feel self-conscious. Keep them for a private high-five just for yourself.

I was flicking through my current journal recently (which is two-thirds full now) and I came across just such a list from a while back. It was unexpected amongst my pages of goals and ideas and I started to read it. I don't mind telling you that I gained such a boost from the list and it really helped to re-motivate me.

I used to think things like this were showing off, but now I know they're not. There's nothing wrong with acknowledging all the good things you've done. It's just another way of knowing that *you are enough* and of keeping your frequency high.

In addition, what you focus on grows in your life, so if you focus on your achievements and things that make you feel happy, then you will receive more of the same. Only good can come from that.

Plans for the year?

What is going on your vision board for the New Year? Instead of New Year's resolutions, why not build some exciting plans into the framework of your upcoming year? They could be:

- Projects you'd like to complete such as writing a book or eBook, or knitting a garment.

- Taking a flower arranging course or eCourse you've had your eye on.

- Decluttering your home, once and for all!

- Becoming slimmer and healthier with exercise and changing your taste palette.

- Reading all the books you own.

As you can probably tell, these are all things that I have on my dream board for next year. Speaking of dream boards, they're a fun way to showcase your desires. There are many ways you can create one – Pinterest is fabulous and if you're fancy with programs such as Picasa (I'm not yet) I've heard that's great too.

I thought I might go old-school for a change and get myself a corkboard so that I can arrange images, quotes and magazine cut-outs with drawing pins. That really appeals to me right now, and my style files have loads of great magazine pages so it will be fun to go through those and display the images that really speak to me.

Vacation time

Something on my ideal Christmas wish list is a vacation somewhere sunny. Because of the way our business is, the only time we can take off more than a few days in a row is between Christmas and New Year, so this works out perfectly.

We always plan something fun; sometimes it's a big trip such as the belated honeymoon (by six years!) we had in Hawaii and sometimes it's local and low-key, like our road trips around the North Island of New Zealand more recently. We enjoyed the summer weather and called into wineries and beaches along the way.

It might not be on the cards for you to take a trip at Christmas-time, but at least think of a few ways you can enjoy a staycation (love that word!) at home or start plans – even if they are far off – for your next vacation. Dreaming and planning is free, and you never know what it could lead to.

Make every day like Christmas

One night a few months ago, as I lay in bed thinking of nice things so I could easily drift off to sleep, I started thinking about Christmas through the filter of when I was a child. It was then that I had the beautiful thought of:

Every day in my life is like Christmas

It's so true! I am blessed to have a comfortable home, a caring and loving husband who is also my best friend, and two comical cats. I never want for anything; if I need something I can go straight out and buy it (within reason of course).

I get to enjoy time by myself and have hobbies and interests that I enjoy. I love reading, and always have the latest from my favourite authors and genres, with free access to our local library and the ability to purchase books and eBooks if I wish to keep them longer.

Without fail, every day includes genuine laughter, smiles, kisses and general silliness that makes me feel youthful and happy. In my life, every day really is like Christmas.

For the most part, this includes that glorious magical feeling of Christmas as well. How?

Because I want it to. No, I don't have Christmas decorations up year-round and nor do I play holiday music out of season. I simply decide that I wish to live a magical and charmed life and go about making it happen, both with my daily decisions and the way I see things.

Like the famous character Pollyanna, if it makes you happy to think a certain way, why wouldn't you? It's not the law that you have to remember all the sad things that you've ever encountered (I sometimes do that and it doesn't feel good). I think there is a balance of being compassionate and aware, without taking the whole world onto your shoulders.

For those of us with 'spongy' energy where we easily take on the feelings and emotions of others, it can be challenging.

If you are the same, it is something that will always be an issue for you to manage, because knowing that you are like this doesn't mean the feeling goes away.

You can protect yourself though. It is helpful not to keep up with sensationalist news and negative stories from around the world. You will always hear about the big stories from someone else, and you can send each situation your thoughts and prayers, along with a heaping dose of love.

You can then focus on doing your bit to make the world a better place by feeling good, shining your light onto others and doing what you can for those around you.

Your thoughts are your happy place, and protecting this happy place is necessary to help you always feel grateful and joyful.

A *chic and simple Christmas* summary

To summarize, here are my top tips for a New Year that is exciting to look forward to:

- Enjoy the feeling of renewal that January brings, by cleaning up your home, and decluttering and organising along the way.

- Spend some time reflecting with your journal – maybe you received a beautiful new one for Christmas, or perhaps you need to put a journal on your wish list? Think through the previous year and make a big love-list of all that you did well, your favourite moments and who you are grateful for.

  As you fill in the pages of your journal each day, you'll find that you feel happier for no reason at all. All the lovely things you are writing down seep into your consciousness and create a lasting effect. When you read back through your journal it will make you feel good too. I like to keep mine by my bed and write in it before sleeping.

- Make a list of things you'd like to do in the coming year. Do they excite you? Do you feel a little flutter inside at the thought of achieving them? From your list, choose the item that feels the best to you, no matter about practicality, and do something towards bringing it into reality.

When I've done this, I'll pick the one I really want and then the voice inside starts up: 'but I should do this other one first, it makes more sense, I already have the materials for it'. You can probably guess that the first choice is the one that has had the best results when I've followed it.

Ask yourself, 'what do I want to do this year?' and listen for the answers.

- If a vacation is something you'd like to do, start making plans. Even if you don't have the money right now, start thinking about where you'd like to go and what you'd like to do. *Feel* how you'd feel if you were there;

flood your body with those good feelings. Sometimes when I've done this, I notice a resistance inside; and that's just the feeling, not even to actually going! I then know it is something I need to work on. Allowing yourself to feel expansive and excited is the first step to making your daydream into a reality.

- Make a decision to have a year-round Christmas feeling, with good cheer, a sparkly feeling inside and a commitment to enjoying life *every day*. Let little annoyances wash over you unnoticed and keep your eye on the big picture – your glorious and spectacular life.

Chapter 7.

Bonus Chapter –
The Christmas 'Best of' from my
How to be Chic blog

This chapter includes my favourite blog posts from previous years on the topic of creating a chic and simple Christmas, plus a very special post; it's a beautiful (and true!) story of a lost pet that I found *just one week* before Christmas.

It really was like one of those Christmas movies, except I experienced it first-hand. I still get tears in my eyes when I think of that story.

I hope you enjoy this Christmas *'Best of'*

chapter.

Plan Ahead
November 2010

At this time of year there are many social events on. In the past I have found it quite helpful to plan ahead what I am going to consume, both food and drink, either on a normal day or going to a party or family gathering.

It's so easy to look forward to an outing as an excuse to eat (and drink) to merry excess, and be fatter the following week. I have had success walking myself mentally through an outing and planning what I am going to eat (or not eat) and what I will drink (or not drink).

For example, this Christmas day which I will spend with my in-laws, I am thinking about not eating any snack foods, chocolates or sweets, no matter what might be nestling enticingly in bowls. That way I will enjoy my mid-afternoon Christmas lunch and dessert.

And because it is likely to be quite warm, I will drink plenty of water and only a few glasses of wine over the meal. I often find wine on Christmas day, a glass here, a glass there, over the day ends up making me feel blah and sloth-like. Definitely not drunk, too much time has passed between each glass, but it makes you want to go to sleep.

I've been rereading my Anne Barone 'Chic & Slim' printouts from her old website – specifically the section on surviving Christmas in a chic and slimming manner. Unfortunately, Anne took all her supplementary writing down when she redid her website recently, however there is still a lot of great information on her new website, *www.annebarone.com*

Anne has some great ideas, like imagining you are a chic French woman spending the holidays with friends. You have been invited to a New Year's Eve party at the home of some locals. Anne says to think about this role; how you act at the party; how you are picky with the buffet, avoiding the processed foods (which you don't understand, being French), and tasting tiny bits of different foods to see what you like.

Because you are French, you don't eat with your hands, so everything you do choose to partake in has to be eaten with a knife and fork, sitting down. You will also remember to keep your posture perfect, and not eat anything that might smudge your lipstick (potato chips can make lipstick disappear within minutes). You will also think about what current events, latest books or movies you wish to discuss with people.

I like Anne's thoughts on drinking: 'Being French, you will also opt for a small glass of beverage of your choice, sipping slowly from it all evening. You won't want to overindulge because then you will not feel well the next day. And especially you will not look your most attractive, if you drink too much alcohol. A healthy look is the basis of an attractive look.'

Some of information in the printouts is from her books, which, if you don't have, I heartily recommend. I have reread mine over and over (and over), and love them. The first three (*Chic & Slim*, *Chic & Slim Encore* and *Chic & Slim Techniques*) are my favourites.

This planning ahead technique also applies to the everyday. I find it quite helpful if I sit down at breakfast and plan what I'm going to have for lunch and dinner, along with fresh fruit (making sure there is some available in the fridge at work) and even things like choosing green tea over black tea, or coffee.

I create a picture in my mind of a day of chic eating and look forward to and enjoy it.

A Serene Season
December 2011

I have decided this year I am not buying into the craziness. I know some enjoy the frenetic buying energy of Christmas, but I am not one of them. I just get stressed and unhappy. And this year 'by rights' I should be more stressed as we are hosting two family gatherings. Other years because we lived in such a tiny place we were always the guests, so why exactly was I feeling so put upon then?

So whether things are stressful or not, I will be calm. I will be happy and 'up' and little things will not bother me. Sometimes it is as simple as making a decision to be that way.

I had planned to keep up my walks and yoga as far along December as possible, but it has been too busy in the shop. That's okay though, I am still calm. Making sure I eat enough protein has been a key factor in this I think. I have been keeping away from junky foods for the most part and planning in a good portion of protein with each meal. It keeps me full for longer and I haven't been craving sugar.

And not eating sugary gross foods means I feel happier and more in balance. Despite there sometimes being an instant connection to eating a bag of candy and then feeling jittery, hot and irritable, I still didn't click and change what I did next time. A friend of my Mum's who is a cancer survivor and is now much more aware of her health stays away from sugar entirely. It's really not good stuff even though it comes along in bright colours and says 'look at me I'm fun, you'll have a good time with me'. And it's marketed at children!

I've also been listening to my good friend Dr. Norman Vincent Peale on his audiobook *The Power of Positive Thinking*. He is a religious man and likes to quote the bible every now and then. I am not particularly religious (I think of myself to be more spiritual) but what he says makes so much sense and it is very calming to listen to him. He really makes me see reason and the world seems a more manageable place after I've had a dose of Dr. Peale.

He says none of us are born as worriers and that it is a habit we acquire over time. We go into it bit by bit and so we have to turn things around in a slow and steady manner. I still have a long way to go, but I am willing to keep doing the work to be a happy and serene person who lets minor annoyances wash over them.

Another way I have been cultivating calmness is to do things ahead of time. Some family members and I swapped wish lists which I have to say I'm a real fan of now. It takes the stress out of gift giving, and isn't a 'surprise' gift a waste of time and money if it is not used? In my ideal world, we would all swap good wishes rather than buy stuff, but who doesn't like to open a brightly wrapped Christmas present on the day.

My relaxed and calm Christmas feeling was severely tested this morning. The first post on this subject I had been writing over the past few weeks went 'pop' just as I hit publish and completely disappeared. Even though I had been saving and auto saving all along, every single word was gone. After checking and rechecking that I couldn't find it, I decided it wasn't worth getting upset about and started writing another one.

And now here I am with a second post. And I'm calm. Today I am at home for the whole day, oh joy, and I can really get stuck in and whip our '*chateau*' into shape.

Be serene this Christmas everyone!

A Christmas Tail
December 2011

I have received a Christmas blessing that is so rich I felt I must share it with you.

Last Friday evening we noticed an odd-looking white cat outside our gate. I very quickly realised it looked odd because it had no ears. That's right – no ears. It was not pristine and quite rough looking and I feared it had been a victim of some kind of cruelty.

Over the years I have given both time and money to animal charities but still remain very sensitive to this, as many others are. To the point that one day I found holes cut out of the newspaper – my dear husband had censored some upsetting stories for me!

Back to White Cat though, she came meowing out from under a car as we walked past. We came back a few hours later and she was still there, calling out loudly. She was very friendly and allowed me to pat her. I brought some meat out and fed her on the grass verge.

The next day we didn't see her and I thought she might have gone home. She was back on Sunday and over the next few days I fed her some more. I realised what a fabulous man my husband was when he suggested we take her in, when that was what I was thinking too.

On a night of torrential rain we brought her inside (we had already been giving her breakfast and dinner) and she stayed the night. She hissed and growled at our cat Jessica a lot but I thought they would get used to each other. She stayed the next night too.

After Christmas, I planned to take her to the vet for a check-up and see if she was micro-chipped to try and track down an owner if there was one, but we feared she may have been dumped.

She didn't look young and when you picked her up she was light as a feather. Quite a difference from Miss Jessica who looks dainty but when you lift her it's like a bag of sand in your arms!

White Cat's ears told me another story though. They didn't look hacked off, but surgically removed, and I realised she may have had skin cancer being a white cat, which would have necessitated ear removal. She looked a little ferrety with no ears I have to say. And I was patting her yesterday morning and my ring got caught on her ear-hole. It didn't hurt her but I felt terrible.

I thought she must be a lost, loved cat if someone had taken the time and expense to have her ears operated on. Plus, she was very tame and operated our cat-door no problem at all. Miss White Cat was no wild cat.

At work yesterday I decided to see if I could find White Cat's owners. First I placed a pet lost and found advertisement on Trade Me (our version of eBay). I rung two vets in the area and asked if any of the cats on their records were white cats with no ears. Then I did an Internet search. One of the New Zealand pet websites with a lost and found section allowed you to search by keywords and areas.

Up came a white cat lost in our area but it had ears. I clicked on the photo anyway and what do you know, the description of the photo said 'this was taken before she had her ears reduced due to skin cancer'. And she was lost in a big park right near us. I couldn't ring the number quick enough.

I phoned her 'Dad' and he couldn't believe we had his girl. She is twelve years old and had been with him since she was six months old. She had hopped into a friend's car, unbeknownst to him of course and the friend drove off. When he got to where he was going (right by our street) she jumped out frightened and ran off and that was the last they saw of her at the end of November. She had been living rough for more than three weeks.

Her Dad came around last night to pick her up. He was such a lovely man, a retired police detective. He said he had tears in his eyes after I rung him to say we had his girl.

I still can't believe it's worked out so well and Dolly has been reunited with her family (her Dad is a country music fan and named her after Dolly Parton 'because she is blonde'). And only a few days before Christmas. I couldn't think of a better Christmas present myself.

And full credit to Jessica for being such an accommodating hostess to White Cat. She did not hiss or growl once, despite a strange cat staying with her. And the nice lady at the cat shelter said Jessica liked her own company and didn't want to be around other cats. Jessica is my true Christmas angel.

I was so happy last night thinking of Dolly and her Dad cuddled up together. I asked him if she slept on the bed with him and he said 'tonight I might let her', and he was planning on locking her in the house with him when they got home.

Merry Christmas to Dolly and her Dad!

A Simple Christmas
December 2013

What excites me most right now is living a simple life, and decluttering and organising to aid in this quest. I've been doing this with many areas of my home and life as I come across them, and a few months ago I thought about Christmas.

Even though it is a time of year I look forward to, there are parts of it I don't like. These things are others expectations and too many gifts. I know I can be a bit of a control freak and that's what I am working on, not being bothered by what other people want or do. I am going with the flow and know that the only person I can control is myself and also the way I deal with things.

I have issues with gifts because even though they are genuine and well meant, I find them stressful because if they are something I wouldn't use, don't like or will clutter my house, I feel like the person who has given me the gift has wasted their money. Being from thrifty Scottish stock that upsets me! My brother calls gifts 'knick knacks and cloggers' and tells us not to give him any. The way he says it always makes me laugh.

And I don't believe you have to give gifts to show love for your family and friends. Little kids, yes, I know get excited about Christmas presents, but as we get older I am more than happy to receive not a single one and just spend time with the people I care about. Last year for the first time my brother, sister and I did not swap gifts and it didn't make Christmas any less special.

So, I sat down to make a list of how I can have a simple Christmas and really enjoy this magical time of year. Here is my list.

How can I have a Simple Christmas?

1. Make a choice to have a simple Christmas.

2. Make lists and look at ways to make items on the list easier/less.

3. No unnecessary rubbish.

4. Don't swap presents with those that agree.

5. Leave time to recharge the batteries.

6. From 1st December switch into Christmas mode – put the tree and decorations up, feel relaxed and Christmassy, watch Christmas movies and television, don't eat too much rubbish – eat good food and feel well.

7. Don't stress about what others will do – take them for who they are and be happy with that.

8. Look at all my Christmas blessings – a wonderful husband, comfortable and happy home, loving family, financially stable, our own business that we happily run together.

9. Think of others at Christmas that I can reach out to – (and I've got a few people listed).

I put our tree up today, and Jessica happily posed for photos. She is such an obliging model-cat. Nina-cat was too busy tearing around to stop for a photo. She never stops! Up and down the hall, in the cat-door and straight upstairs, s-shape from the dining area, down the hall and into the guest bedroom and many other routes. I wonder if it's because she grew up from kitten-age in a crowded cat shelter until past the age of two with no room to run around – she's really making the most of all this space with just her and Jessica now!

With my decluttering enthusiasm lately, I even managed to declutter my Christmas tree decorations. I tell you, there is no part of my home that escapes decluttering at the moment.

I realised the purple decorations I bought a few years ago which I thought would zazz up my Christmas tree were a big mistake. I am not a purple girl. I am classics and I am neutrals.

So, I took out all the decorations I love and put them in a smaller container and bagged up the purple hanging baubles and purple tinsel and put them with the coloured fairy lights. I donated these to a charity store today when I went out. When I want something gone, I want it gone.

Now my tree has a petite collection of Christmas decorations on it, in silver, gold and a touch of red; and white fairy lights. I also have a few decorative items around my coffee table candles and apart from these, just a small wreath in our entrance way (and I'm even a bit half-hearted about that so it could be donated soon). And that's the extent of my simple Christmas decorating.

Christmas Chic
December 2013

Now that Christmas is almost here, have you planned ahead on how you are going to most enjoy the day?

Having been a little bit strict with what I eat

and drink in December (just a little, not completely strict, that way it's do-able for the long term), I also plan to not let myself go completely on Christmas day. I have a plan for what I will consume, and while this sounds a bit Bah Humbug, I know I will be happier both during (looking chic) and after (feeling chic and slim).

Something as simple as deciding what you will do beforehand makes it surprisingly easy to resist temptation later on.

For example, I know that sugar makes me feel horrible after I've had it and I often end up with a sinusitis headache if I've eaten lots of sugar in one go (the headache can last 2-3 days or even more). You'd think I would learn, and perhaps I am now.

I am not talking about natural sugars here. I have fresh fruit every day for breakfast and am happy with that. But processed sugar is another thing altogether and I know I am happier with it not in my diet for the most part. Enjoyment of life is important though, so I have some sweet treats most days (like two squares of 72% cacao chocolate after dinner).

On Christmas day, my plan is to enjoy my meal and not pig out on nibbles beforehand, and have a small dessert after. Often the first taste is the nicest, and once you have tasted it then what do you need more for? At least that's what I'm telling myself, and doesn't it sound more chic than a piled-up dessert bowl?

We have two 'Christmas days' coming up. I am doing desserts for both Christmas dinners. For the first one on Christmas day, I have been asked to make a Banoffi Pie. This dessert is decadent to the max, so my plan is to have the tiniest sliver after my dinner, so I can have a taste of it without making myself feel sick.

The next Christmas dinner one day later, my plan for dessert is to prepare fresh seasonal fruit and bring a gourmet ice cream to have with it. Doesn't that sound refreshing after a big Christmas dinner? Remember it is summer here!

I have plans for drinks too. I will be taking along chilled bottles of Perrier and sparkling white grape juice and will sip these from a champagne flute. I don't drink anymore but when I did, I would often have only one glass of champagne before dinner and maybe one glass of wine with dinner.

Drinking during the day makes you so tired, even one glass will. I still remember a champagne Christmas breakfast where I had a couple of glasses of bubbles in the morning and felt out of sorts all day.

And to finish off, you may also want to think about plans on how you are going to go about your Christmas day. What time you are going to wake up, how organised you will be, how relaxed and cheerful you are and how much time you will leave yourself to get to places. When I have a social occasion coming up I like to do this, and it helps me be calmer, nicer and enjoy it more.

I also pledge to myself that I will have mystique and decorum when I am there, and always, always have a strategy to deal with those that I know may challenge my serenity. I don't want to stoop to their level so I try to take the high road and don't do much of the talking myself; that way I cannot be caught out by them. I am pleasant but detached around those I am wary of.

I realise my strategies outlined above may seem like overkill and a bit regimented but they aren't supposed to be. I just like to think about things beforehand and go through likely scenarios and how I will react to them. I also like to play out dinners in my mind and think about what I will eat and drink. There is a quote about discipline setting you free, rather than holding you back like we think it does, and I try to remember that.

Deciding about things ahead of time really does help me be disciplined and do what *I* want to do, rather than be carried away with what's available and what people offer me. You don't need to make a big deal out of not having something either. If someone offers you something that you don't want, you can simply say, 'oh I couldn't right now, but I might have some later when I have a bit more room', or if it's before dinner 'oh I'm saving myself for dinner, I might have some later though' (later may never come but no-one needs to know that!). And of course, a simple and polite 'no thank you, I'm good' with a smile always works too.

I always find it's easier to resist the first taste of something you didn't know you wanted until you saw it, than to try and stop that automatic arm shoveling snacks into your mouth.

Lastly, pull your shoulders back and remember to breathe. I have to constantly remind myself of that.

Relax, it's only December

December 2014

Now that it is December, how are you feeling? Have you suddenly become overcome with panic like I did earlier on this week? I literally had trouble breathing for a day or so when I realised it was only a little more than three weeks until Christmas Day. It felt like a tightness in my chest that made it difficult for me to take deep breaths.

Thankfully I feel much better now and am almost breathing normally again (I can be so dramatic at times). On Tuesday, I had a day at home so I started by listing out everything I wanted to do up until the weekend. I thought I'd take things week by week.

We have an early Christmas dinner at our place this Saturday night, so there was the house to clean and make look nice, a Christmas tree to decorate and grocery shopping to plan. I also had to pick up my great-aunt from the airport and her flight was delayed (which I found out about when I arrived at the airport). Since it was at least half an hour until it even landed let alone get everyone through customs and security, I had the bright idea of doing my grocery shopping at a supermarket right near the airport rather than the one nearer to our house. I was very proud of my canny time management!

Throughout that day and this week as I got my breathing back to normal, I reminded myself that 'there is no hurry' and that my mindset preceded my experience, so I could choose to be calm and not let my mind spin off into 'I've got so much to do and I don't even know where to start'.

The rest of this week I've done more things on my list and I think pretty much sorted my Christmas gift purchasing. It helps that I have simplified this list quite a bit with family members that agree not to exchange gifts.

I've re-read my 'A Simple Christmas' post from last December and I am pleased to say I am doing all the things I suggested. And I feel tranquil and serene! Listing everything and then going through the items one by one is the way to go. And taking deep, soothing breaths.

The Importance of a Good Routine
December 2014

Working in retail as I do and have done for the past ten years, it is expected that December can get a little nutty. Yes, even in a shoe store which you wouldn't think is traditional Christmas fare, but we do get a lot of people shopping for gifts (thank you customers!)

Being extra-busy in December means I have to be organized and keep my calm. I cannot freak out too much about not having my housework days and be content that the house is tidy. I need to organize meals ahead of time so we don't resort to takeaways that make us feel crappy. I have to have my Christmas gifts purchased and wrapped so I don't have a meltdown on Christmas Eve when we've just arrived home from work and SURPRISE! Christmas is the next day.

Currently when we get home after the store has closed, it is all I can do to put on a load of washing and make dinner. I'm just keeping up with the basics and am okay with that. My half hour of reading with a flute of bubbly (non-alcoholic for me thanks) before we eat dinner is my haven of rest and calm.

I think it is because I have been working on establishing a good routine that I have handled December reasonably well this year. My daily walks that I actually look forward to because of my iPod Shuffle have continued, and only dropped off this week because we are working longer hours. I can't wait for Christmas day though, so I can go for a nice stroll before breakfast.

I don't think we've eaten one purchased meal at all this month which is a minor miracle in itself. Instead, starting off the day with fresh fruit, good yoghurt and raw nuts; having our fridge at work stocked with salad vegetables, nice salad dressings, hard-boiled eggs, leftover roast chicken and back-up cans of tuna for a yummy and filling lunch; and then home for a light and delicious dinner with loads of steamed fresh vegetables.

Eating good stuff makes you feel so much better than eating what I used to consider treat foods. In September, I was diagnosed with celiac disease and have been eating gluten-free since then, which immediately cuts out a lot of pre-prepared foods. This has made me more aware of what I put into my body and what the results are, as in how I feel after I've eaten something.

I had a biopsy to confirm my celiac status and it was a gastroscopy where they put a delightfully long tube into your mouth. I could see my insides on a television in the hospital room, those lovely clean and pink tubes and it made me not want to pollute them with plasticky faux foods. I tend to forget what I've eaten as soon as I put it in my mouth. I would never consider what effect it was having on my body other than a nice taste. Well I've had my eyes opened now!

I'm not saying my diet is perfect and I still love to eat something delicious and rich, but it comprises a smaller part of my diet now, and my treats are higher-quality for the most part.

Another important part of my normal routine is my favorite sleeping hours – 10pm to 6am, and I have kept these up too. This has helped enormously in keeping me happy and sane, and I am sleeping like a log because our days are so full, which is wonderful. Not being able to fall or stay asleep at night is the pits, and I credit my daily exercise in helping with this, as well as not gutsing myself with sweet treats at night (sugar hypes you up, as any parent will tell you).

Minimal television is another big thing for me. At the moment I watch about half an hour in the evening, preferring to spend the rest of my time with a book or magazine, or listening to an audiobook when getting ready for bed.

I was listening to a great interview with Brian Tracy recently (you can find it here: *https://soundcloud.com/coachmike/goals-2014-with-brian-tracy*). Brian suggests taking a minute each day to write out your top ten goals in present tense. Over time some goals will change, and some will remain on the list; it keeps at the forefront of your mind what you want to focus on. I think this is a great idea and today I will get a jump-start on the New Year by commencing this habit.

Seeking simplicity?
December 2015

When I think about what my core values are, a word I keep coming back to is simplicity. It's not that I want to live my life in an empty room with nothing and nobody around me, but when things get too busy, whether it's the contents of my home, my schedule or the thoughts in my mind; it doesn't feel good to me. What feels much better is having space in all senses of the word. Space to move around, space to breathe, space to think and space in time.

I think the most important thing for us to consider is just when that feeling of discomfort kicks in, when our internal compass is telling us 'it's getting crowded'. If you ignore that voice it is easy to start acting out by being snappy with people, eating when you're not hungry and deciding to go shopping because a new something will make you feel better. I identify with all these things.

Knowing now that I have a core value of simplicity means that I can take action much sooner, and one day I would love to be able to simply 'be' in simplicity all the time. I know that it's not something outside of me though and that I can have simplicity any time I like, even right now. Making the *decision* to have a life of simplicity marks a point where everything else flows on from.

For me, a life of simplicity would contain plenty of time to get all my jobs done and still have time to read, potter and play. It would also mean that food is enjoyable nourishment and not my main source of pleasure (because I have other things for that).

There are many ways I can bring these ideas into being. The discipline of being organised is not pushed aside, because it feels good when I have things under control. Taking actions on small and big things as they arise, with no procrastination, is key. Every piece of paper I don't action whether it's to file, throw out or make a phone call for, represents a leak of energy. You know that slightly heavy feeling of little things undone?

Not trying to pack too much into a day is another way I can cultivate the feeling of simplicity. And then doing those few things so that I feel proud at the end of the day.

Simplicity in food means there is a feeling of peace. I am not trying to avoid certain foods to be skinny, rather, I am choosing not to buy and eat certain foods because I don't feel well afterwards. That feels far more empowering to me.

Simplicity of the mind means not overthinking things. When my brain is whirring like a runaway train, how blissful it feels to stop and think 'all is well, I am enough, life is good, I am safe today and always'. I can then think 'what is the next step, what do I want to do next'.

That might be what the feeling of simplicity boils down to – taking things one step at a time, doing a job as it needs to be done with no multi-tasking; finishing something I have started and feeling satisfied with a task completed.

It is especially important at this time of the year when we have more to do and less time to do it in. List everything out, pick the first thing to do and just start with that.

A word from the author

Thank you so much for purchasing *A Chic and Simple Christmas*. I do hope you have gained some good ideas that you can implement into your holiday season and beyond.

My Christmas wish for you is to *enjoy your life*. To enjoy life whilst living with others around you. To be happy to wake up every day and look forward to that day with gusto. To enjoy the happy days and the quiet days, the mundane days and the days where exciting things happen.

Treasure yourself and the ones you love. Whatever you are plan to do over the holiday season I hope you have fun.

Be positive and excited about making simple changes in your life – you can do it! Jump into the driver's seat and steer this Christmas and the New Year in the direction of your dreams.

I welcome feedback and would be grateful if you could leave an honest review at amazon.com.

Please join me for weekly inspiration on living a simple, beautiful and successful life at *HowToBeChic.com*

Thank you,
Fiona

About the author

Fiona Ferris is passionate about, and has studied the topic of living well for more than twenty years, in particular that a simple and beautiful life can be achieved without spending a lot of money.

Fiona finds inspiration from all over the place including Paris and France, the countryside, big cities, fancy hotels, music, beautiful scents, magazines, books, all those fabulous blogs out there, people, pets, nature, other countries and cultures; really everywhere she looks.

Fiona lives in beautiful Auckland, New Zealand, with her husband, Paul, and their two rescue cats Jessica and Nina.

To learn more about Fiona, you can connect with her at:

howtobechic.com
fionaferris.com
facebook.com/fionaferrisauthor
twitter.com/fiona_ferris
instagram.com/fionaferrisnz
youtube.com/fionaferris
bit.ly/FionaFerrisBooks

Fiona's other books:

How to be Chic in the Winter: Living slim, happy and stylish during the cold season

Financially Chic: Live a luxurious life on a budget, learn to love managing money, and grow your wealth

Thirty Chic Days: Practical inspiration for a beautiful life

How to Live Well - Chic Inspiration - How to be Slim and Healthy (3-in-1 book)

How to Live Well: Simple and practical inspiration to enjoy your everyday life

Chic Inspiration: Imaginative ways to live a more magical life

How to be Slim and Healthy: A French-inspired journey to slimness and good health

Made in the USA
Middletown, DE
29 July 2017